Bohead Paid For His Own Funeral

Bruce Buckner

Dedication

So I want to dedicate Bohead Paid For His Own Funeral to everyone trying to make it out of the hood. To everyone working toward a better life. To everyone working to build generational wealth for their family. Thank you for supporting me as an Author.

Bohead Paid For His Own Funeral is for the individuals stuck in the hood. In the penitentiary around the world. You have the power within yourself to change your life. Really praying for this book to be a life-changer. Suppose Bohead Paid For His Own Funeral inspires you in a positive way.

Also, I would love it if my readers showed more love for life. Kill all hate in life. Live more positively, and most importantly, use your time wisely.

Yours sincerely, Bruce Buckner.

Business in Nashville

Website

www.BruceBuckner.com

Phone number 901-463-8211

Email address:

bucknerbruce414@gmail.com

Lip Gloss, backpacks, phone cases, and more for Teenage Girls.

www.Brukiya.com

Lip gloss, backpacks, leggings, and more

www.Brucoya.com

Credit Builder Link

(http://self.inc/refer/10163812)

Clayton Fleming

Number 615-686-6855

atyourservicejanitorial@outlook.com

website

www.atyourservicejanitorial.net

Contents

Dedication   2

Chapter One   6

Chapter Two   15

Chapter Three   25

Chapter Four   35

Chapter Five   45

Chapter Six   54

Chapter Seven   65

Chapter Eight   74

Chapter Nine   84

Chapter Ten   100

Chapter One

Bohead Paid for His Own Funeral.

It all starts in Haynes Garden Apartment, one of the most dangerous neighborhoods in Nashville, Tennessee. One way in, one way out. The people in these apartments were ruthless, even the women.

Bohead was an only child. Being an only child, Bohead developed a strong sense of independence. Bohead was also wise beyond his years. Bohead was very intelligent. He made sure that he achieved whatever his plans were once he set his mind on achieving a goal. He had a strong sense of creativity.

Raised by a single strong woman, Bohead was sensitive toward women. He loved to kiss and hug his momma. The two would sit and talk for hours, which helped Bohead develop strong verbal skills. Dirty Red Bohead was momma's street name. He was raised by a hustler, gangster, a master of all trades. When it came to living in the streets, granddaddy has been in the streets since before he was a teenager. He always had a pocket full of money. Whenever he came over to visit, Bohead's granddaddy would hand him a $100 dollar bill. **"Save this grandson,"** he always said.

He was a gangster fly in so many ways—a real boss. Everyone in the city knew Bohead's granddaddy. Everyone wanted to live like him, and Bohead always wondered why. One day, while in the breezeway chilling with the big homies, granddaddy pulled up in a blue Rolls-Royce with a three-piece matching suit. He was flying as a muthafucker. He was dressed like a mobster. **"I see you, granddaddy. You look like Al Capone. Walking like John Gotti the Teflon Don."** Bohead said. **"Grandson, I'm more like Big Meech."**

You could see that my granddaddy's suits with the hat to match. It was of the best quality. Bohead wanted to be just like his granddaddy, but what did granddaddy do for a living.

One day, I decided to get a piece of my favorite snake. Homemade rice Krispy treats. My momma with her daddy was at the table. It was money, a big bag with Lemon Pound Cake on it, and a triple beam scale. Bohead's granddaddy sold cannabis, straight from California, cream of the crop.

While the two were handling their business, Bohead opened the oven to cut a piece of rice Krispy. There was no going back to your room, Bohead. Nothing was ever hidden from me. Bohead's momma and granddaddy always kept it real with him while growing up. After a while, during a conversation that my momma and Granddaddy were having, I found out my Granddaddy was fronting my momma, the Lemon Pound Cake. Dirty Red sold the weed straight out of the apartment. It was life every night. With females and niggas coming in and out of our apartment. Every one of the customers was breaking Bohead off with a few dollars. Saving the money I collect was installed in Bohead at this time in his life. One day, Bohead saw that his savings had stacked up, **"I do not even know how much money this is."**Bohead said

Bohead got the shoe box and took a seat on his bed. It was a whole hour before I stopped. Having a hundred dollars was a lot to me. Plus, it was all $1 bills. Just imagine how Bohead felt. It was exciting to him to have a knot of his own.

Bohead was so excited. He decided he wanted to show off the money he had saved. Bohead made a choice to take the money to school. At this time in Bohead's school career, he was in the 2nd grand, going to Amqui Elementary School.

At lunch was the time for Bohead to shine. While paying for lunch because I was not on free lunch, I pulled out the knot of a $1 bill to pay for it. The Lunch Lady noticed the knot I pulled out.

Bohead being wise beyond his age, knew the money was going to get the Lunch Lady's attention. What Bohead did not know was money brings haters too.

Bohead finished eating his lunch and went back to class. After a few minutes later, the next thing everyone heard was, **"Bohead, come to the Principal's office."** The teacher plus everyone in my class knew I was in trouble for something from the tone of the Principal's voice.

Once I arrived in the Principal's office. **"In here, Bohead."** I heard from the corner office. Soon as I walked in, **"Bohead, where did you get all that money you got?"** Said the Principal. My pocket is full of money because I have been saving my allowance. My parents give me from doing chores around the house.

What I told the Principal was a cold-blooded lie. The dollars were from two days of customers giving breaking bread with me.

"Let me see the money, Bohead?" As the Principal, I pulled the knot of $1 out and handed it to him. He counted my money with a tasteless look on his face. The money had coke on it. Some of the bills had blood on them. The Principal knew it was street money.

After counting all the dirty $1 bills, the Principal came up with a new rule in Amqui Elementary. And the rule was students could not have that amount of money. **"Sorry to say this, Bohead, but I have to take this from you. This is too much money for you to be walking around school with."** What he said made me the maddest kid on Earth.

Because now, my pockets were empty. At that moment, Bohead vowed not to ever let someone take money out of his pocket. Bohead's whole day at school was bad. He started to act out in class. Every hour the teacher was saying, **"Raise your head up, Bohead. No sleeping in class."**

"Bohead, stop talking and focus on your work. Bohead, get that frown off your face." "Go get my money back from the Principal," was my response. Whatever the teacher asked went in one ear and out the other all day long until the final bell rang. Bohead was giving her a hard time.

Once I got home, my momma said the Principal had called her. And that your money will arrive in the mail. **"You do not have to** be mad now, Bohead; I'm gonna give you your money back."

"I know you will, Dirty Red," Bohead said back to his momma. She went off on me, **"Don't you ever call me Dirty Red again, you hear me?"**

Bohead was still mad at the Principal for making up new rules on him. No work was turned in until the $1 he took from my pocket was back in my pocket.

Bohead even started skipping classes. Some mornings, he would walk out the door like he was really going to school. Bohead would even walk toward the bus stop just in case his momma was looking out the window. Even though he knew she was asleep.

Haynes Garden Apartments is surrounded by woods. Every kid in the garden had a secret place to go in the woods, also known as a clubhouse. My clubhouse was located between Haynes Garden and the Duplexes.

It was a dirt cut that was engraved in the ground from all the people running through it. No sunlight could shine on the area. Plus, big homies use the cut to get away from the police. When a raid was going down, this cut was used for many things.

On the right side of the path was a big tree, which I loved to climb to hang out. At the trunk of the tree, it was blown out to look like a cave. A lot of the time, Bohead was underneath the tree, looking for tadpoles and bullfrogs.

It was my clubhouse, my quiet place. I would spend hours in the cut. Before Bohead knew it, he would see kids walking to their apartment. Yes, school is over, I would say.

To your surprise, Bohead was never worried about getting in trouble for skipping school. Mornings, afternoon, and some of the evening, my momma was always sleeping, being up all night smoking, drinking, and serving all her customers. Plus, she was holding a big pistol on her side. It was a lot on her body, which turned Bohead's momma into a vampire. Dirty Red came alive at night.

All the gangsters were coming to our apartment; they were like giants to me. Bohead looked up to them so much because they looked out for Dirty Red. No other man was able to even come see my momma or any woman living in Haynes Garden Apartments. Gator, Micheal Stewart, Wesley, Ivan, and Killer Charley, were known around the city for running. Niggas who came to Haynes Garden to visit the women right back from where they came.

Chapter Two

Killer Charley eventually got caught with a body and was sentenced to life in prison before he was 21.

Every weekend all of them homies would go to different neighborhoods to rob the biggest dope dealers. One weekend, Killer Charley decided to kill one of the dope dealers by shooting him in the head. He was later caught from his handprint on a doorknob.

After each robbery, our apartment was the place they came. It would be money, drug, and gun all over the living room floor. Every robbery, they would give my mother tens of thousands of dollars; these guys were very protective over my momma and me. Once finished, all the bigger guns were placed somewhere in one of the closets in the back of our apartment. Once they left, Bohead ran straight to the back, looking in the closets to play with the guns he just saw them put away.

Bingo Bohead found one wrapped in a black shirt. Dang, this thing is heavy. Bohead was now pulling the trigger of a loaded Uzi, though not yet strong enough to make it go off. Message; very dangerous without the safety on.

This was the first gun he ever picked up around the apartment, and it won't be the last one.

It was Bohead favorite time of the year, Christmas. Every Christmas, Wesley would come over to put together the toys my momma bought for me. All Bohead's toys were the coolest.

Dirty Red spent a lot of money on Bohead's gifts. She would get the most expensive race car track, ice hockey table, and 3in1 arcade games. Wesley would be over for hours, putting the toys together.

He would even stay over for hours playing with Bohead. Sometimes he enjoyed playing with the toys more than Bohead, which was funny to Dirty Red.

"Wesley, take your old azz home and let Bohead play with his toys." She said, laughing. Wesley left only to come back with a Nintendo that has no Christmas wrap.

"Bohead, this for you," Wesley said. **"What is it?"** I asked. **"This is the new Nintendo game that just came out. You play it on the television with remote controls."** Wesly replied. At this time, floor model television was the thing. So it was difficult to find a channel that would work.

The first game Wesley put in the Nintendo was Iron Mike Punch-out. Bohead and Wesley were up all Christmas night playing the game. Not able to last until the morning. Bohead went to sleep in Wesley's arms.

Bohead woke up to see that he was all alone. He started playing Iron Mike Punch-out. Bohead could not beat Mike Tyson for the championship belt. Bohead was getting madder each time he made it to Mike Tyson and then lost. Bohead got so mad that he broke the remote control. He pulled the cartridge out of the Nintendo, opened the screen door and slammed the cartridge to the ground. Getting mad and having a hot temper is what Bohead learned from

Killer Charley, Gator, Micheal Sterwert, Wesely, and Ivan. This time, Bohead's temper got him in trouble with the homie. **"Dirty Red, why is the game I just bought in pieces on the breezeway?" "Bohead got mad because he was not able to win a Championship belt from Mike Tyson."** Wesley started laughing, knowing it was hard to beat Mike Tyson in the game.

Bohead could hear his momma's conversation with Wesley over how the game got broke. Bohead started smiling when he heard his big homie laugh at him.

Every Easter, Bohead, Clay, and Pacman would get animals from granny, which is Pacman momma. This particular Easter, Bohead was gifted two baby ducks. Clay was gifted six baby chickens and Pacman, a rabbit.

One evening while watching the ducks swim in a manmade pool, Bohead started to get too rough with the baby ducks. Bohead picked one duck up by the neck and forced the duck's head under water. The duck was trying desperately to get loose, but Bohead was just too strong for the baby duck, which eventually led to the death of the baby duck. Bohead placed the dead duck by the pool.

"Bohead, what is wrong with you? You just killed the duck your granny bought you!!!" Yelled Dirty Red. **"No, I did not; the duck drowned,"** Bohead said back.

Dirty Red just walked off from Bohead, so she would not get madder than she already was. She got on the phone to call all Bohead's friends to have a duck burial.

The whole breezeway was full of my friend and their parents. We all walked to the woods to find a place to bury the duck. We all got in a circle bowed our heads. **"As we come here today for the dead of Bohead's duck. Almighty, the Great Physician. You have blessed Bohead as a steward of this beloved duck for many days. Bohead made a few good memories through your grace and greatly enjoyed his time with the duck. Yet, you give, and you take away. You are**

good in all things, so we give you thanks and praise. O Lord, bring healing to Bohead's broken heart. Help him to get through this season of grief."

Amen.

Bohead made eye contact with some of his friends. Some of them were smiling because never in life would we think we would have to show up to a duck funeral, but they did.

One thing about the people in Haynes Garden Apartments was that we loved, supported, and cared for each other. Everyone in Haynes Garden Apartment has got into a fight with one another. It did not matter how hard we fought to hurt each other. We will always become friends again.

Bohead decided to visit his cousin, Clay. Knock, knock, knock, Donna, open the door for me. **"Clay is in his room playing with his chickens,"** she said. Bohead, why have you not been coming to school? The Principal took my money the other day. When I get it back, you will see me in school.

Bohead's cousin, Clay, had a temper too. Clay and Bohead were playing with his six baby chickens. One chicken just was chirping too much. **"Stop all that chirping,"** Clay said, trying to scare the baby chicken. Annoyed that the chicken did not stop, Clay picked the baby chicken up by one leg then started swinging it in a circle. It was the funniest thing I had ever seen. My aunt, Donna, came in to stop Clay from killing the chicken.

After all said and done, the baby chicken suffered a broken leg.

Clay was living in a different household than me. Donna, Clay's momma, was very strict. She will discipline us in a minute. Well, not me. I always ran from the whippings. Not because of fear; I just did not like to be hit on because my momma did not whip me. Anyway, Clay also had a good stepfather named David, which gave him a father figure to look up to. Their household was more traditional. It was also my cousin, Trina. Bohead was always getting in trouble for kissing on Trina's cheeks. Trina had the fastest cheeks.

Bohead finally got the hundred dollars the Principal took back in his pocket. It still was unfinished business that had to be handled.

Bohead was still feeling some type of way when he saw the Principal.

You know what? I got to get revenge on him and the Lunch Lady. It will happen in an open area with the two together. Something got to be done. No one took from the big homies; my big homies did the taking. Bohead thought to himself.

This being Bohead's first time putting in work on his enemies. He has not learned at th time that it involves activities such as strategic planning and strategic thinking.

Bohead was a wild young boy. Once off, the schoolboys. Bohead walks to the store right across the street from Haynes Garden Apartments. Even though Bohead had a game at home, he did not have Street Fighter, so he got a few quarters to play the arcade version of Street Fighter.

This was one game that Bohead got really good at. It was a few hours before Bohead was out of quarters. An idea came across Bohead's mind. Piss the Principal and Lunch Lady down. Yeah, I will throw piss on them at lunchtime. Bohead walked to the back of the store where all the drinks were; Bohead picked out his favorite drink, which was Kool-Aid Burst grape.

Damn, the hole is too small for me to piss in; a 20oz Sprite bottle will work perfectly.

Bohead poured all the Sprite out while walking up the hill to F Building. Bohead went straight to the refrigerator to place his Kool-Aid Burst up for later. I walked to see if momma was there because the house was so quiet, but Momma was still sleeping as usual. Well, I will get ready for tomorrow. Going straight off instinct, Bohead walked to the bathroom to take a piss in the Sprite bottle for tomorrow. He filled the whole 20oz Sprite bottle up to the top, Bohead put the top on, washed the bottle off, and placed it beside his bed.

Morning could not come fast enough; Bohead had been up all night twisting and turning, thinking about the mission he was about to complete.

Bohead was more enthusiastic about getting ready for school this Friday. Before leaving for school, some inspiration was needed. Bohead walked to the closet, where he saw the Uzi, lifted up a few shirts and shorts, and there the Uzi was still wrapped in the black shirt.

"Dang, this gun is heavy," Bohead said while walking to the bathroom with it. Bohead looked at himself in the mirror for a few seconds. Bohead raised the gun and pointed it at the mirror.

The Principal and Lunch Lady magically appeared. No Bohead, do not do it. Bohead pulled the trigger, and blood went everywhere in the bathroom. Both their bodies fall slowly to the ground. Bohead blinks, realizing that it was only his imagination.

Inspired now, Bohead put the gun back exactly how he found it. Got the Sprite bottle to put in his backpack, then headed out the door to the bus stop.

Chapter Three

The bus had arrived right in front of the double doors entrance. It was 7:30 in the morning. Lunch was at 12:00 noon. As each hour passed, the piss was getting louder and louder. Bohead's classmates smelled it too. Every time someone walks to the locker. All I heard was, **"It smells like pee back here."** A few students started walking to the locker area, then walking back to their desk with a hand over their nose.

Shoot, I hope Ms. Green does not walk to the locker area. My mission will be a complete failure; I do not want that to happen. Then

I would be letting down my big homies. Thoughts ran through Bohead's mind.

Lunch was taking forever to come. The whole time Bohead was on his best behavior. Bohead did not want to bring any heat on himself at this time. He was even more active in class by raising his hand and asking questions, solving problems before other students.

Finally, the bell rang, which only meant it was lunchtime. Every student that brought lunch to school walked to the locker area. The rest of the students walked to the door to line up. Once most of the students were away from my locker, it was my chance to go get the Sprite bottle full of piss. Bohead placed the bottle on his hip like it was a Glock 40. **"Will you please hurry up, Bohead,"** said Ms. Green. **"Be right there. I am grabbing my lunch money,"** Bohead said back. Also irritated for being rushed.

Bohead was the last student in line. Ms. Green was in a hurry to get us back to class to test us. She's gonna say I need you all to finish your lunch fast. We have a 36 question quiz to take.

We all looked at our friends like what! Knowing we were not going to be eating fast to get back to a 36 question quiz. Ms. Green should have kept that to herself.

After telling us about the quiz, she opened the door and started walking toward the cafeteria. We had to walk past the Principal's office every time we went for lunch, this gave Bohead a chance to glance inside to see if the Principal was in there.

The Principal was making his rounds around the school, which means he was most likely intimidating all the students in the cafeteria. No student likes to see the principal outside the office.

Soon, as we entered the cafeteria, Bohead saw the Principal standing on the far wall. At first, it looked like Bohead was not going to be able to piss on the Principal and the Lunch Lady down at the same time. **'This mission has to go as planned,'** Bohead thought. It starts coming together as planned as the line was moving, the Principal was moving closer towards Bohead.

This Friday, the cafeteria was serving pizza, corn on the Cobb, turnip green, and fruit cocktails. While Bohead was getting his food placed on the tray, the Principal was now talking with the Lunch Lady.

Bohead's blood really started boiling as the two looked at him. As Bohead was walking toward the two knowing what was about to transpire, an unpleasant feeling came over him.

With not much time on this Earth, Bohead knew from this moment forward that the feeling he was experiencing was not that of a killer, and it had to be overcome with action?

Bohead was getting closer as each student walked to a table. While pushing the tray with one hand, Bohead was pulling out the Sprite bottle with the other, needing a few seconds to unscrew the top; Bohead placed the bottle on top of the tray to do so. The time was now; the Principle and the Lunch Lady were a few steps away. One more student was in my throwing range. Not wanting to get any piss on the student, Bohead had to wait a few seconds before going in full acting mode, acting like he tripped over his shoestring. While tripping toward the

Principal and Lunch Lady, Bohead squeezed the bottle of piss on them.

The Lunch Lady screamed at the top of her lungs. **"Bohead, that was piss in that bottle!"** **"It is in my mouth!"** Everyone in the cafeteria was laughing. It was that funny.

Everyone in the cafeteria was laughing. It was so funny Bohead even had a grin on his face. That grin went straight away. Once Bohead saw the Lunch Lady charging for his neck, the Principle grabbed her just before she could lay a hand on Bohead. **"Bohead, go to my office now! Do not stop act take with no one. You are in big trouble this time!"**

That Friday was the end of Bohead's school career. The Principal kicked Bohead out for the rest of the year. He made a call to his momma to tell her Bohead would receive his last report card in the mail because he would not be allowed on the school premises.

Bohead was surprised when he walked in the door and saw his momma sitting on the couch, face redder than a dash of red pepper. **"Bohead, why did you throw piss on the people? Do not answer because I**

know damn well I did not teach you to be like that toward others. That was fucking trifling of you! Go to your room before I go upside your head! No playing that damn game until I say so!"

Bohead went to his room, put his backpack in the closet, and lay on the bed to think. Bohead could hear all his friends playing outside at the playground. The positive part was Bohead could see them too if he looked out the window.

The following day while everyone his age was in school, Bohead heard some shooting close to his window. It was Dion chasing someone with a gun. Dion was faster;

 Because he caught the guy in the breezeway, then shot him in the ass. It was confusing because the guy he shot was from Haynes Garden too. A few minutes later, some more Haynes Garden homies walked up. They were shaking each other hands now. It was a game; they were playing hide go shoot. Bohead thought the game was a myth just floating around Haynes Garden Apartments.

Bohead has been seeing the game Hind Go Shoot played from his own eyes as historical.

The big homies did play a game called Hind Go Shoot, which consists of one team having a certain amount of time to hind. If you were on the team without a gun and caught, you were shot in the ass. Haynes Garden was a rugged crib to the fullest.

It was around three weeks when Bohead's momma walked into the house with the mail. **"Bohead, your report card came today." Come to the kitchen to get it. Alright, give me a second. I'm putting my money up." "Boy, I know you've been counting that money all day." "You're right, momma; my new obsession in life is counting money,"** Bohead said, stashing the knot of money away. **"Hurry up; you can get back to counting your money later. This is more important right now. Do you want to see if you were going to the three grade?"**

"Yes, I want to see if I passed," Bohead said, reaching for the envelope. Bohead saw his last 2nd-grade report and had the worst feeling a student could feel. The following year Bohead will not be going to the 3rd grade. That means bitch, Ms. Green failed me. Bohead was traumatized; he did not want to attend school anymore.

Failing 2nd grade sparked the entrepreneurial spirit in him, the thought of investing the two hundred dollars stash in his Nike shoe box. Bohead's momma could be messing sometimes. There were sandwich bags full of yellow envelope bags in a giant zip lock bag underneath my momma bed at all times.

Since Bohead decided not to go to school anymore, he was gonna jump off the porch to hustle full time. "**Yes, selling marijuana gonna be my career,**" Bohead said.

All around Haynes Garden Apartments, is Dirty Red got that killer? Yes, Bohead momma is the plug.

All Bohead had to do was sneak one of the sandwich bags from the closet. Place his two hundred dollars inside the giant zip lock bag.

Moving forward with the move, Bohead put the play in motion. He found a picnic table where most of Haynes Garden Apartment's traffic was at. Bohead started waving his hands to the cars, which is what he saw the big homies do. No car was stopping for him.

Soon, hours passed without catching a single marijuana sale. People must be looking at me like I was a crazy dude out in the streets, waving cars down to stop. Bohead was determined to become a great hustler. He thought about how he will be written down in Haynes Garden Apartment's history books of hustlers.

Even though days went past with one purchase from someone. Bohead kept on trying, but one day, Bohead got some action. It was a Saturday night when Bohead noticed a Burgundy G Wagon; it was lit up driving up the hill. It was the cleanest SUV Bohead have ever seen. The burgundy G Wagon pulled right up to the picnic table where Bohead was posted.

The windows were tinted, making it hard for Bohead to see who was in front of him. Bohead did not like that the people in the G Wagon were just sitting in front of him. That made Bohead get up to walk and walk in the opposite direction of the G wagon.

The passage window finally came down.

A female voice yelled out. **"What a boy your age doing out here by yourself?"** Excited that he was not in danger. Bohead answered, **"Selling marijuana!"** **"Is that right!"** the passage commented. **"Well, I want three**

dime bags.” Bohead walks a few feet from the picnic table to his hiding spot to grab the three bags for her. As Bohead was getting closer to the G Wagon, all the females in the SUV were smelling the Lemon Pound Cake. **“This Lil boy got that killer!”** Lexus said, looking around at her sisters, Brazil, Africa.

Lexus had already counted the money out for Bohead and had hit hanging out the window for Bohead to grab.

Bohead grabbed the thirty dollars so aggressively that Lexus was turned on sexually. **“All yeah, thank you for the purchase,”** Bohead said to Lexus while walking back to the picnic table. **“Where are you going? I want to introduce myself to you.”**

Chapter Four

Bohead was in deep thought about his first transaction as a marijuana seller that he did not even hear Lexus. Once eye contact was made, Lexus signalled Bohead to come back to the G Wagon.

"Lil Homie, you gone have to pay attention while you out here. You did not even hear what I said to you." "What did you say to me?" "Being a businessman, you gone have to take time, get to know your customers. I want to know your name." "My name is Bohead." "Bohead, my name is Lexus." Lexus looked at her sister, which was a signal for her to introduce herself too. She leaned forward and said. **"I am Africa; nice to meet you, Bohead.** The back window came down, and another female said. **"My name is Brazil. Like the country." "Alright, good to meet you all too,"** Bohead said.

Bohead did not know that meeting Africa, Brazil, and Lexus was the best thing that could ever happen to a nine-year-old kidpreneur. Bohead will later find out.

Africa pulled off, giving the G Wagon some gas so its engine could roar. Africa saw in Bohead's young eyes that he really liked the SUV. Africa was right; Bohead was now on the picnic table, daydreaming about how he would look driving the G Wagon. If he could make it to eighteen years old.

Growing up in Haynes Garden Apartments had Bohead thinking he would not make it to the age of eighteen. It was just that ruthless in the Haynes Garden Apartment, also known as HGA.

Lexus handed her two sisters the sacks of Lemon Pound Cake. **"Damn this some killer weed,"** Brazil said from the back seat.

Bohead knew nothing about the danger that came with hustling.

"Sit, Lexus, what do you think about Lil homie out there like that?" Africa asked

He's just a child right now; yeah, he's just a child out there with the wolves," Brazil said. **"I like him,"** Africa's sister intuition was taking over. What would momma say if a little brother was thrown to the wolves momma would be turning in her grave?

The sister took a liking to Bohead that night. It did not sit right with any of them that Bohead was young, hustling with weed.

"Let's go home to talk about this some more sisters," Africa said.

Africa had a huge mansion she bought from being an entrepreneur for so many years in a library; was a huge round table placed there for business meetings and to have important conversations and, last but not least, plan.

The sisters decided that night to become Bohead's mentor. They're gonna coach him and keep him focused on his hustling career.

The next day, Africa, Lexus, and Brazil rode through Haynes Garden, looking to buy some more killer weed from their little brother.

Bohead was sitting at the same picnic table with his money out counting. The sisters did not like that because, at the same damn time, they said, **"he's slipping."**

Bohead looked up and saw the G Wagon in front of him; Bohead waited for the window to come down.

"Bohead," yelled Africa, who was on the passenger side of the G Wagon this time. **"You're not excited to see us, Lil brother."** **"Yeah,"** Bohead said, noticing she called him Lil brother, **"so you all gone be my big sisters? This Lemon Pound Cake brought you all back to Haynes Garden?"**

"My sisters and I been thinking about you a lot Bohead." What are you all thinking about me for? I am good in the hood." "That is what we have been thinking about. Bohead, you have no idea how it really is being a hustler. These city streets can be murderous. What you say the name of that weed you got?" "Lemon Pound Cake!" "That is the best marijuana in the city."

"Listen, Bohead, other niggas from other parts of this city will be envious of your success and see you as a problem."

"Problem, what kind of problem am I causing Africa?" Asked Bohead. "With the brand, you are selling Lemon Pound Cake, Bohead. Will make their customers start spending money with you, which will stop them from feeding their family. It is a lot to the life you are choosing."

"Listen, sisters, Haynes Garden is my Kingdom! No one going to fuck with me plus the wolves out here, my big homies."

The real reason Africa, Brazil, and Lexus was in Haynes Garden was to purchase all the Lemon Pound Cake Bohead had to sell. With no marijuana to sell. He will have to find something positive to do.

"How much Lemond Pound Cake you got in your bag today, Lil bro," Africa asked?

Bohead walks to his stash to grab his bag so that he can count out how many yellow envelope bags were there

Africa saw that the sandwich bag was stuffed with yellow envelope bags. **"Come sit in the back seat, so no one will notice what you're doing, Bohead."**

While Bohead was in the backseat, Lexus and Brazil said, "What's up little brother and gave Bohead a hug."

"What are the hugs for?" Bohead asked. **"We are just showing love; don't worry about it." "Thank you, sisters."**

Bohead poured all the bags on his lap; one-by-one, he counted the yellow envelopes while placing them back in the sandwich bag.

"Africa, I got 50 bags." "Ok, I want to buy all of them." "Really," Bohead said with much excitement in his voice.

"Yeah, but Bohead, you're going to have to find something positive to do for the rest of the day." Okay, I will, Africa, I promise.

A sister could really see his age now because they all looked at each other with that look when you pick up a cute baby.

It was a must that Bohead keep to his words with his newfound sisters after Bohead counted the $5 hundred dollar bills that Africa gave him.

"Thank you, Africa, for buying all my weed. I will always keep my word. So I'm going

to keep it real with you. And go over to the homemade basketball court to play basketball with my friends."

Bohead walked over to the woods where all of the kids in the Haynes Garden played basketball; one of the kids really loved basketball; he had to create a cut-out for the rims and two pieces of flat wood for the backboard.

Once Bohead got on the court, he took a seat on a large tree that had been cut down; it was a few of my friends sitting on the homemade bench. Who got next on the court, my uncle Pac-Man was in the woods pissing. I did not even see him, Bohead I got next you can be on my team

"Ok, Uncle, what about the next two players?" "They're playing four on four. Playing basketball in the Haynes Garden can be very intense; no one likes to lose; it's always that one person that gets mad and kicks the ball off the Dirt Court that makes the game not so fun because it was a water crack that was running a couple of yards away from the court. Playing basketball on a Dirt Court with a wet basketball was not fun.

We could all be walking home super dirty from the house of playing.

Bohead was really loving his new business; his money was really stacking up only because Africa, Brazil, and Lexus were coming into the Haynes Garden every day to cop his whole weed stash. The sisters were already changing Bohead's life for the better. Bohead's momma was noticing her money was stacking up big time. Bohead was hearing her say, **"Where did this two hundred dollars come from?"** while playing his video game.

Being an entrepreneur is much better than going to school; I probably won't use most of the things teachers are teaching in the real world.

Every day for years, Africa, Brazil, and Lexus were pulling up in Haynes Garden apartment to buy all of Bohead's weed; that plan of action kept Bohead safe for years. As a matter of fact, it was a whole nine years

But it all went bad on Bohead's 18th birthday; one of the Haynes Garden's big homies was killed. Michael Steward was a giant that many niggas from the other side of town were scared of him.

Michael Steward was out east, buying some bricks from a plug he met through a female. Michael wanted to make sure the coke was right.

So he cut one of the bricks open to snort; this was his way of seeing if some glasses were mixed with the coke.

It was a setup; some of his enemies paid the female to lace the bricks with rat poison. Michael Steward was rushed to the hospital, where his lungs collapsed.

Then, not even an hour had passed that the ambulance was pulling up to the G. building; Wesley had been shot six times in the breezeway by a girl he was cheating on.

Bohead was so upset at the event involving his big homies; he made a choice to set every dumpster in the Haynes Garden on fire; the police were called.

Bohead was arrested with charges as on reckless endangerment, property damage, refusing a direct order.

Bohead was taken to TriStar skyline medical center for his injuries which consisted of a broken arm, black eye, and bike marks from the K-9.

After what the police did to him, Bohead made it a mission in life to get every police officer that put their hands on him.

On top of breaking his arms, the police officer went in his pocket and took the $5000 Africa had spent with him early that day.

For some reason, the money that was taken was not in his book. One day at the medical, Bohead's name was yelled out, **"What is this?"** The letter stated that my money had been seized, and they slapped a possession to distribute marijuana charge on Bohead. It was a new tenant that's been watching Bohead. Snitching was not allowed in the Haynes Garden.

It was not long for the words to get back to Wesley, Ivan, and Charley, aka Big chew, that the tenants that snitched on Bohead were living in building no 273; the snitch door was kicked on and gunned down.

Chapter Five

The snitch booked a one-year lease by moving out the next day. Haynes Garden niggas were known around the city because there were ruthless over there. The Haynes Garden niggas who scared the shit out of you when they are active.

Bohead went to court every other month; it was always something going on with the defence team witness. The first two Court dates were set for later dates for COVID-19 testing.

Every time Bohead went to court, someone on the defense team tested positive for covid-19, so the judge was stating that everyone who was dealing with a defense had to wait for the colleague that was out as a result of covid-19; court day was always set for another day because of the virus. The virus caused Bohead to stay in the Justice center for a whole year. The Justice center is one of the worst places in Nashville to this time. On May 4th, the judge sentenced Bohead to a 6 months program.

It was a facility 35 minutes from the Haynes Garden. Apparently, almost every gangster and gang member in Nashville has been to CCA. Sam, a guard, worked around the unit, waking inmates up for transportation. Bohead was one of the inmates when it was time to go to the CCA.

After 2 years of hard time, Bohead was leaving the premises. Lexus ass better be put there waiting for me since it has been 5 months. I stopped her from coming to see me; she was upset when I told her to stop driving down this way. I had to remind her how a whole family got killed by an 18 wheeler. The family was headed to see a family member in the penitentiary. I box shit to feel from here on out; it's either get down or lay down. Where the hell was Lexus on the day I got out? She was not there on time; damn, that's some backwards shit.

That must be her in this stretch Hummer; Bohead smiled, knowing that was her seeing the Hummer pull up and park. Bohead could tell it was more than Lexus in the truck, both of the doors opened. First her, then my niggas, Dominique and Markel. The guards in the parking lot coming to work looked in amazement. **"Bohead, I see your big ass over there trying to hide; come on." "Ha, ha, ha, I was gonna try to scare you, now you see me nigga. I know you don't think you can hide behind that tree bush or whatever; you then got fat as hell."**

"Yeah, Bohead, you big nigga, I see they feed you good in there," Markel said. **"Yeah, it's cool but not better than outside food." "Take me somewhere so that I can get something to eat." "It's whatever, where you want to go? Hmm, subway, that's just where to put something in my stomach while we ride, bro. They got you all the way down here in red necks land,"** Dominique said and burst out laughing. **"It's too damn far, ain't it?" "Hell yeah, nigga too damn far." "Nigga, you better stop saying nigga before you see 5 or**

10 red necks come running this way with pump and ropes and shit."

Everybody burst out laughing, walking to the truck after that joke, hopping the black Hummer truck stretch. **Damn, this truck is clean as hell." "It had to be your idea to get this, wasn't it?" "Yeah, I like this." "You already know I had to come get you in style."**

"Where is my baby at?" "He is at your mother's house; Lil Bohead looks just like you too. Wait until you see; you're gonna be in amazement." The whole time, the 3 of them laughed and talked on our way back. The ride was comfortable; the Hummer had all types of entertainment inside of it. Riding past downtown, everything was almost the same; the only difference was more buildings.

There must be some type of business buildings." "Some of them are; the others are condos. "Where are peaches and Susan at?" "At home taking care of business. Tomorrow, your mother and I will be cooking dinner for you; my girls will also be there. We figured we'd do something the

day after you get out. I know you are going to the mall, and that's what all the other staff niggas did when they got out, but I know you better not but their fucking hoes." What, Lexus has never come at Bohead like that.

All of you must be super emotional about our relationship since the baby was born. Bohead laughed, and Lexus shot him an eye that was so serious and said, "I'm not playing. Fuck that; you are staying home with me." "Ok, but I'm going to the mall first; I need to be clean. Take me over to my momma's house." "Where do you think we are going? You know she couldn't wait until you got out, Bohead. She got Lil Bohead spoiled with lots of pampering." "Why do you say that?" Bohead ask. "She is always picking him up." "She is gonna have to stop that; my Lil nigga gonna be hardcore." "Bohead, you are not gonna be teaching him that." "Yes, I'm gonna need practice." "Ha, ha, ha!!!" Markel and Dominique had to laugh on that one.

"You serious, ain't you, Bohead?" Dominique asks. "You already know." Lexus stood there looking at him, knowing she wasn't gonna be able to stop him from teaching his son all that Haynes Garden Apartment (HGA) lifestyle. Just to get underneath his skin, she said, **"Lisa can spoil him if she wants to."**

Bohead shot her a look that could have killed her. Thinking to herself, I love doing him like that. Sometimes just sometimes, you have to pick with him. Walking into the house, Bohead said, **"What's up, momma?"** Heyyy, Bohead, I'm sure glad you out this girl was a real couch potato for real. I don't believe that he looked at her with a look, saying, I can't wait to get you in the bed. **"Where is Lil Bohead at?"** **"In the room, sleeping. Don't wake him up."** **"He's my Lil boy; how are you gonna tell me not to wake him up?** Bohead said, walking, looking for the room he was in. Lisa had bought herself a new house to live in after doing so well at her place of business. **"Where is he at with all these damn rooms?"** Bohead walked in, seeing his boy sound asleep.

He looked at him for a second, catching his pewters, then gave him a rough kiss on the cheek, waking him up after a few of them and picking him up. Lil Bohead looked at him as so to say nigga; I'll kill you when you wake me up like that. **"Yeah, he is my son,"** Bohead said to himself, walking back to the living room with him in his arms.

"There he got my Lil nigga; he looks just like you, Bohead." "You think so? What size of clothes does he wear, Lexus? I want to take him shopping with me." "He got plenty of clothes. He does need some shoes." "Never mind, I'll just take him with me." "Ok, but it's gonna be hard after some hours have passed. He's gonna get crying. You gonna have to feed him too, plus you gonna have to change his diaper when he shit." "Damn, all at that? Just right his sizes down for me."

Before I take him out, I'm gonna get to know him first. I will be back, Lexus, stay here. I'm going to the barbershop first. I don't need any nigga's giving you the eve.

She walked in the back, shaking what her momma gave him. **"Bohead, don't be out there doing anything right this second; chill for a couple of weeks. A lot of things changed since you were gone,"** Lisa said, giving her son lecture about the streets. Bohead figured that it had just been a two-year difference. "I want him to take long before he was fully back in the streets again. The three of them all left; the first place was the barbershop masters peaches on Clarksville highway. When three of them walked in, all eyes were on them. Dominique and Markel James were gleaming, plus their gear was up to PO. Bohead's old barber motioned him to get in the chair. **"Damn, Bohead, you are a beast; I haven't seen you in a while; where have you been?" "I'm fresh out from doing two years."**

"So, what're your plans, my nigga. You are already now back to the basics. So, you still be having the weed?" "Nah, I'm chilling right now; this shit kinda tight for me right now. I'm on community connection; this shit is serious." Whatever you do out there in the streets, be low-key." "Yeah! Yeah! I'm gonna do that." Bohead looked in the mirror, likening what he saw. **"Yeah, I see you haven't lost it." "I haven't looked at myself in a good mirror in a while."** Another barber came in while Bohead was getting out of the chair. **"What's up, Bohead? I haven't seen you in a minute." "I had been down 2 years." "Here, go to diameter, one of them Big Meeche, the other one, Lil Booster, you**

gonna like them." "How much?" "They are free."

Damn, Bohead liked that, knowing he hasn't got anything free in so long. **"Alright, you, I'm out."** Markel shot him 25 dollars, then they left. Bohead wondered, then asked, **"How long do we have the stench hummer truck?" "Just for the day." "I like this; it makes us feel like a star. We gonna have to keep this for a week. I can't wait to pull in HGA with these." "They gonna think we Baby lil way or somebody. We can't. It doesn't matter to me." "Yeah, let's keep it for a week or two,"** Markel said. They told the driver the next stop was Hickory Hallow mall.

Chapter Six

Bohead saw a couple of his old girlfriends; Bohead quickly walked into the mall and grabbed his pair of shoes, 2 pairs of Air Jordan, and the other ones are Air max, plus five outfits to match, and a cell phone then they left. They rode around town, getting up with niggas picking up money and letting them know the boss was back in town. Now they could get back to their business which was taking over the United States drug trade. The cartel really didn't expand much while Bohead was down.

"Most of the money was coming in from the factory they already took over; it was

like five states, we already had 45 more to go." "Ok, you, I'm ready to take it on in Lexus, probably at home having a fit." "I'm thankful for having friends like you."

"You were taking care of business when I was away. My money never came off short. Then I came home to 300 thousand in a daffy bag. That's real; it's 100 thousand over. My nigga did well. Tomorrow we have gonna have a cartel meeting. I'm gonna set up the next shipment from Sosa. I want you to call all the niggas we have at home, let them know we are having a meeting at my momma's restaurant, and make sure to let them know to be there on time. I'm gonna call and give you the time of the meeting."

"All yeah, it feels good being home." Bohead exited the truck and walked into the house. "Where is my Lil nigga at? That better not be him back there crying." Bohead walked into the room where Lexus was changing his shitted diaper. She picked him up, trying to stop him from crying. Let me see him. She gave Lil Bohead to his daddy; to her surprise, he stopped crying. "See, he stopped crying; he knows his daddy already." Lexus gave him a look that said, you are the man. She noticed Bohead was holding him right in a comfortable potion. **"Yeah, I know how to hold a baby. It's a natural thing." "A natural thing. So how do you feel being at home?" It feels real good. It's gonna feel even better when you give me some pussy."**

"I'm not giving you pussy now." "I do need another baby right now." "Stop playing before I put him down." "Put him down." Then Bohead laid him down in his baby crib. He grabbed Lexus and picked her up like a fifteen-year-old girl, spinning her around. **"Stop, Bohead, stop. I don't particularly appreciate getting dizzy." "You gonna give me some coochy then." "Yeah."** He laid her down on the bed and got between her legs. **"No, Bohead, not here; your momma is in here." "So it ain't like she doesn't know we do it. Nah, it won't feel right; you know you will have me making all kinds of noise." "Ok, then, just let me feel it then."**

"Hurry up." Bohead stuck his hands down her pants to get a good feel; it was tight as hell. He thought it was gonna be bigger since she then had their son. **"Ok, that's enough; I'm getting horny already." "Let me stick it in one time." "No, because you gonna get**

carried away, just wait until we get home." "Come on, get Lil Bohead and his stuff; let's go; I want some of my peaches."

"Give me Susan's number. I need to talk to my man." "615-485-9134." Bohead dialed the number, but no one answered. 5 minutes later, his phone rang. "Yo, someone called Susan." "Yeah, what's up, my man." "Who is this?" "Bohead, you forgot my voice after 2 years." "My man Bohead, when you got out, I had been home for a few hours. I already know why you called; I'm out of town taking care of business as we speak. I know you've gone for 2 years. So you know I got to do something for you so that it's gonna be like you never messed a dime. The price is a lot cheaper. This is what I'm gonna do for you."

"I'm gonna give you a truckload full of cement. You still know how to lay bricks, don't you?" "Yeah, yeah, I'll never forget how to mix and lay cement."

"Susan, before you send me the truck, I want to have a lil fun while I go to freshen up outside." "Give me 2 weeks; then I'll be ready." "My niggas were sending me a lot of pictures while I was down; they went to the Bahamas. Lexus got one of those packages my niggas gave her when they came back. So that's where I'm gonna be for a week. Next, I'm gonna chill in Las Vegas; when I get there, I'm gonna call for my load." "That's cool; you don't need to jump right back at it anyway, lay back and enjoy your freedom. I'll be back in Nashville in the next three days. If you haven't left, give me a call so I can come see my nigga."

"Alright, my day one nigga." After that, the call was ended; some minutes later, they had the most intense sex they'd ever had. They lay in the bed sweating, with Lexus placing her head on his chest. **"You still got that package my men gave you, the one where they went to the island." "Yeah, I still got it. It's lying in my closet on the floor in the corner."**

"How long will it take for you to set up the reservation for the cruise?" "We'll be able to leave in 4 days." "Come on, let's get up and get on that." "What about Lil Bohead, is Lisa not gonna want to watch him?"

"He's not being watched; he's coming with us. I need to spend some time with my Lil nigga." Alright, that's so sweet, Bohead." "Don't think I'm gonna be a slouch as a father. He's gonna love his daddy, watch and listen to what I'm telling you. You see, the first time I picked him up, he stopped crying. He felt the roughness in me." "Whatever, Bohead, you think you are all that?"

"Not yet; I haven't been out long enough to think that." "Where are my girls at?" "They are at home, don't worry, you gonna see them. They will be at the restaurant. It ain't nothing in the world that can stop them from missing your momma's macaroni chess. Everybody loves my momma's cooking show. Your homies always want your momma to have lasagna on the menu." "For real?" "Then, some good friends you got, they always ask how you are doing or if you need anything; they always come on time with your money." "We homies, we can always depend on each other. I'm glad you brought them up while I was down."

"Dominique's momma died. She did Bohead! Yeah, I think she got real sick or something." "He never said anything to me about it. Dominique doesn't talk much. He keeps his family business to himself while we are still one family; I got a family member getting out the pen in a few months. He has been down for 11 ½ years." "Damn, what did he do to get that much time?" "Mike!!! Mike was doing all types of shit in jail. He would've been home a long time ago." "Bohead, what's your plan on going once you meet your goal." "Soon, I'm gonna put a diaper clothesline out for women, thick ones like you, Lexus."

"You then got phat since you had our son." "Bohead, would you say something like that to me!" Lexus was heated; she hates when someone comments on her weight. "**Not fat! Fat, but phat PH.AT.**" "**Ok, that's more like it.**" She then got real sexy supermodel sexy. Thick in the right places. "**Lexus, you look real healthy-looking.**"

"We both look grown and sexy. It's gonna be fun that we are taking a trip, as this will strengthen our relationship." "Because it ain't no telling what you were doing when I was gone." "Don't go there because you know I was too busy running around for your ass." After their conversation, they went their ways. Bohead poured himself some bathwater. **"Damn, it feels good being home. I haven't taken a bath in 2 years."** Bohead sat in the Jacuzzi tub thinking about his meeting with his crew. It's been a while since they talked. Bohead didn't keep in touch with the other members.

That's was Dominique and Markel's job. Since he was gone, she went into the guest room on the internet, getting things ready for the cruise they'll be going on in 4 days. While doing so, she decided to call Peaches and Susan. Peaches picked up on the third ring. **"What's up, girl? Why did you call me so late?" "I'm gonna tell you. Call Susan on 3 way so I can tell y'all at the same time."** Peaches clicked back over; they were already talking about something that went on in their day. Susan didn't know Lexus was on the other line.

"Girl, what is it that you are talking about. Listen, you, this beautiful redbone woman came into the spa today, she was breathtaking. The woman had a real exotic look. Her face was filled with freckles. She was short but real thick, and she knew it because you could tell this by how she

walked. But anyway, she had on this badass two-piece suede suit she told me she made it herself."

"Her name is Meeche; she's a fashion designer. I got her number. I was thinking we could adventure into a new field of work. We could put her down with us. Well, that's all I wanted to say." "So what's up with y'all." Lexus spoke up. "Guess what I got myself today?" Both of them asked at the same time. "What you got?"

"I got some dick Bitches!" "What! You cheated on Bohead." "Hell no, I won't ever do that." So how did you "get some then? He is out; I went and got him this morning." "You drove down there by yourself." "I didn't drive at all. His boys and I rented a stretch hammer. Well, he's out; I called to let y'all know Lisa's cooking dinner tomorrow at the restaurant at 5. So be there, because he has been asking about the both of you. You know y'all are his girls, so don't let him down."

"Girl, you know we are coming. I'm not missing Ms. Lisa's cooking." "Lexus, that was a dumb question." Peaches said. "So,

what do you think about the girl, Meeche?" Susan asked, thinking about her in a sexual way, knowing she wouldn't mind getting a taste of that. Susan knew she could turn the woman out. **"It's ok with me,"** Lexus said, **"but make sure you do a full background check on her. We don't need TBT, FBI running up on us."**

"We then did a lot of shit to get to where we are today. So we need to be really careful about the people we come across." They all said they love each other, blew kisses, and hung up the phone. She hollowed out, **"Bohead do you want a suite or a regular room?"**

"Lexus, you know I always want the best. You are acting like you don't know me anymore. I was only gone for 2 damn years. Nothing much has changed about me but my dick size. You feel good about that to PA little. So, what you think about my newfound skills? Do I make you nuts when we are sexing?" "Yeah, all the time." "Cook us something to eat, Lexus." She went downstairs while Bohead stayed upstairs with his son. An hour later, she came back upstairs with two plates in her hand. **"Damn,**

Lexus, you cooked all this?" The plates had steak, potato, and a salad. **"Where are the drinks?"**

"I couldn't carry the drinks downstairs." She walked back down to get the drinks. The both of them ate a late-night meal and watched movies till 2 in the morning. The two of them woke up early in the morning. Well, really, Bohead woke up first, still in that jail time. Two hours later, he woke Lexus up to fix both of them breakfast. **"Listen, nigga, don't be waking me up all early and shit. I'm not on that jailhouse time!"** She woke up snapping, but she still went downstairs to fix both of them breakfast.

Chapter Seven

One hour later, little Bohead woke up crying. His daddy walked into the room and picked him up. He stopped crying and smiled when he saw who it was. **"You like your daddy being home, don't you? You must be hungry, too, huh! Come on, yo momma's downstairs fixing you a bottle now."**

The both of them walked downstairs, where Lexus was standing in the kitchen, getting his food at the right temperature. Lexus handed Bohead the bottle. **"Turn on the TV for me, Lexus. You can tell that my son loves me already." "Did he stop crying when you picked him up? "Yeah, why were** you just asking?" "Bohead, you see why you need to get out of the game. You have something to live for now. I would hate for something to happen to you again." "Like what, Lexus?" "Bohead, you can get killed out there! You are not Mr. Untouchable, Bohead. You could have been killed before. Where are you going with this? It's niggas just like you out there trying to get where you at." Bohead went off; he didn't like her letting him know one day, any day, he could be killed. He knows what it's out there in the mean street to real young. It was so much happening in my house hood.

"I used to pray to God to let me live until I was 18 years old. I always wonder how I would look when I was grown or how it would be to be a man. Now that I'm here, I don't need you to remind me that death is just around the corner. Telling you the truth coming from the heart, I'm not scared of death." Lexus didn't say anything else to him. The three of them relaxed until it was time to head over to Lisa's Soul Food. To Bohead's surprise, the place was packed. He, Lexus, and the baby walked inside. It was family members, but most of the people were part of his crew. To his surprise, it was every one of the members, even the ones in the five states they had already concerned.

Bohead didn't know that Lisa's momma had a surprise for him, but before she surprised him, they all ate a big dinner. **"Can I have your attention, please? This is to my son, my only son. Bohead has come a long way from where we come from. I don't like what he does. And he knows that."** Bohead sighed and looked at his momma. Ms. Lisa looked back, "Well, I don't, but without you, this place wouldn't be here today. **"Thank you. Come on, y'all, follow me."** They all got up and followed Lisa. She led them into the kitchen, and in one of the freezers, she was met with this question. **"What is all this, momma?"** She didn't say anything. She just opened up a secret door on the floor. **"Come on."** She walked down first and cut on the light. When they all got down there, everybody was amazed at the sight. It was laid. There was a big oak table in the middle of the room, with 6 big leather chains around it.

It was a leather section in the corner of the room. Two big flat-screen TVs. One for watching TV and the other one with a surveillance system for watching what is going on around and inside the building. Lisa also got a huge fish tucks built in the wall, one with sharks swimming around and the other one with red belly piranha. **"This is for you, Bohead." "Ok, momma, let me put the room in use."** Bohead and his crew all took a seat. The ones close to him were seated at the table. Just when Bohead was about to start talking, knock, knock, knock. He looked up at the surveillance camera, and a smile came across his face.

Peaches and Susan were standing, waiting on Bohead to open the door. He opened it and said, **"Damn, what took you so long to open the door. It seems you don't care about seeing us." "Nah, I'm mad at you two." "Bohead, you haven't seen us in 2 years. Yeah, I know, so why do y'all have to come in here late." "All that's why you mad at us. We are sorry, Bohead."** They both planted little kisses all over his face.

"I'm gonna make it up to you, ok." Peach said. **"Ok, fam. Let me finish talking to my crew." "Alright nigga, you didn't have to say it like that,"** Susan said. Then the both of them went back upstairs. Bohead's eyes remained on Susan, noticing the extra fat she had shacking behind her. **"Ah, Bohead, what's in that refrigerator over there?" "I don't know." Go see; I'm just getting out." "You are asking me like I have been down here before."** One of the crew members opened it. **"Damn nigga, it's full of crystal."**

"Bring everybody in; we need a toast," Bohead spoke firmly. **"Here's a toast,"** he said, raising his glass with his Jacob watch, full of diamonds, glistening. **"To the men who weathered the storm. The men may not have made it to the shore, or if they did, some still have a lot to learn."** He looked around the room. **"But the cartel is still standing, and we're still here to tell the story to us."**

Each crew member popped open their crystal bottle. They all chilled with their Bossman for a few hours or until their phone rang. Bohead was waiting on Sosa to show up, but he didn't. Bohead could understand because a man in our line of work always is. A few more hours passed, Bohead was downstairs by himself watching BET. He didn't mind; he wanted to catch up on his videos. While sitting there thinking, watching, and flicking through the channels, his Granny and old memories came to thought. While Bohead was doing time to be exact, I was in my 11th month. She had really started going downhill. Considering my circumstances, they gave me a 3 day pass home. It felt so good to be going home, but it all changed when I walked into my Granny's house. It didn't seem right looking at my Granny like that. She had all kinds of tubes coming out of her. She was in a coma. She wouldn't open her eyes, but she would talk to you. They had her on a breathing machine that was by her side.

So much had changed since I had been gone. Walking in the house from almost watching another charge. Fucking around standing on the block, the damn police rode up on us. It was packed all in the yard. That they didn't see it because guns were on their minds. I can't lie; my nerves were shot to the roof. The only thing on my mind was taking a shower and watching a lil too.

I decided to go talk to my Granny, but it was so hard because I never thought Granny could be so down. Trying to think of something to say brought tears to my eyes. I just stood there thinking but how it's gonna be living life without her. The only words that came out of my mouth were, **"How long will she live, is she gonna make it to Christmas?"** The nurse said, **"Nah, her system is shutting down. I found something in her pee today; I'll give her a few more weeks."** Standing close to my Granny, I could see she was trying to say something. Getting closer, she was trying to say, Happy Birthday Pac-man, but it wasn't his birthday; it wasn't until another week. Pac-man came in an hour or so later. I told him that Granny tried to tell him Happy Birthday, she must have known she didn't have a long time because she died 3 days later. The funeral was on my Uncle Pac-Man's Birthday. It had to be the saddest birthday he ever had. But to me, I wasn't as sad as seeing her suffer. I felt good at my Granny's funeral because she was at peace. I knew God had her with Him. She was the best Granny on Earth. It was time for me to get back to my destination. That was the worse feeling that I have ever felt. I said my goodbyes, and that was that. I was on the interstate headed back. I had a couple of grams of pure white cocaine in my ass; that's how we get it in.

Transportation came and got me at the house. I really didn't want to just go back like that, but Lexus talked me into it. Bohead came back to himself when his phone rang. **"Yo, who is this!" "This is Susan, Bohead; where are you? I'm in town." "You know where my momma's place of business is." "Yeah!" "That's where I'm at." "Ok, I'm headed your way now." "Ok."** 15 minutes later, he was downstairs talking to Bohead. **"The trade will be here tomorrow at 6.00 pm. Do you have someplace to unload the 3 thousand birds?" "3 thousand birds!!!"** Bohead said, excited, knowing it will be easy to get a billion dollars if they keep hitting like this. **"Yeah, I told you that I was gonna make it like you didn't miss nothing. As soon as you finish, I'll have another 3 thousand for you." "You didn't forget that I was going to the Bahamas for a week." Bohead, my memory has just fucked up; it was just a couple of days ago when you told me."**

"It's good that you are going because that's a big shipment right there. You gonna have to go real hard to get it off fast, but take your time, Susan. I need this because I spent a lot of money while I was 2 years.

But now that I'm back, I'm taking over the world one city at a time with every nickel and dime."

The remainder of the day, he, Lexus, and the baby sat at home, getting everything ready for the trip. They'll be going on the next day. They had to be at the airport around 10.00 am. Everything was new to Bohead. Well, not new; it has just been a long time since he had been on an airplane. The night finally ended; the three of them were on their way to MIA. It seemed like it was all new to Bohead, but it wasn't. The only thing new was getting on this big ass strip. The strip was like an underworld on water. It had everything on it, clubs, swimming pools, casino, etc., the strip was super nice, but the water was even nicer. The water was a beautiful, blue and dark blue places light in the other. I had my phone off because we needed to know our destination. It was us against the world.

Chapter Eight

Me and Lexus were having the time of our life. We had to video everything we were doing. If it was just drinking at the bar, one of us had the camera. We had to take turns because babies were not welcomed. Nah, I'm gonna say it like this. We wanted to have our little alone time. The people were beautiful in the Bahamas. The air was even clearer and fresher. It made me want bigger and better things out of life. I did a lot of thinking while on the trip. I knew once I got back home, it was back to the basics. And that was taking over the United States.

My own personal dope house. I say that because once I get to that level, I'm gonna have homes all over the globe. So get ready, America, because here I come with full speed ahead. We were on our way back to MIA, straight to the mall to ball and strip for a minute. It didn't take anything but an hour to get a few things. I didn't really need much, but I did get a lot; it was a habit that I picked up over the years.

We really did it by for Lil Bohead. I got him a few in-and-out pieces to wear when we wanted to show him off. Yeah, that's right because he's gonna be something else, but one thing I'm gonna try not to do is involve him in the drug trade. I'm gonna make sure he goes to the best schools.

We gonna need a close family member to keep the legal business moving when we get to the older numbers of ageing. Who's better than our own son. When the three of them got seated on the plane, Bohead turned his phone on, and it rang. **"Yo, who is this." "This is Mike Mike."** He was excited to hear Bohead's voice. He has been calling all week. **"I'm already out. I have been out a week now." "They gave me an early release.**

I'm on the plan now, headed your way." "We can chop it up then. I got something for you. I'm gonna make sure you're seated properly."** Once they hung up the phone, it didn't take long to arrive home. The three of them were walking into the house. **"Lexus, you and Lil Bohead gone back to the door. The hinges have been kicked off. "Damn, somebody kicked in my damn door! Fuck."** Bohead was mad as hell. He ran upstairs to see if anything was moved. The fifteen thousand, well, a dumbing chunk he had in a shoe box was almost visible and easy to get to. That way, the robbers would leave quickly. The other half of the 300 thousand was in a secret safe under my rug in the closet. That was all there. Bohead grabbed his chrome 44 magnums that he had stashed with other guns. He walked back out the door and locked it. Bohead would see she was on the phone with somebody. **"Hold on, girls, he is "walking to the car now. I'm just gonna call you back when I see what's up." "Somebody broke into the damn house,"** Bohead said, with bleeds of sweat on his nose and forehead. **"Did they get anything?" "Yeah, the room is messed up. It's shit all on the floor. The bed is flipped**

upside down. The money I always have in the shoe box is gone." "What, they got all that money you came home with when you came home? Nah, didn't you listen? You know damn well I don't keep all our money in one spot." He said, not knowing she was offended.

"Why you got an attitude with me deep down?" Bohead thought she might have something to do with it. Knowing that it was 300 thousand dollars in the house, but that thought quickly went away knowing how much they had been through, plus I wouldn't even be at the level I'm at if it wasn't for her. My fault; my mind is moving 100 miles right now.

 "Have you brought anyone to this spot that might be those of you?" "None that I can think of. All yeah, a couple of new people moved into the 2 empty condos across the street. How do they carry themselves? The house on the right, I have only seen them folks, a few times from their looks, they are eating pretty good.

The house on your left got some natty-looking people be coming over. They like to

snap around. One time when I was coming home, they were looking around my next-door neighbor's yard. Two to three hours passed, I saw the police over there. I put it on everything that they had something to do with our house being broken in." "All right, I'm glad you told me that; I'm about to get on some real killing; I think I haven't put in work in 2 years. I need some blood on my hands. I'm gonna kill them real slow. They broke my door and entered my damn house. I got something real nasty for them." Bohead didn't forget that he handed a gallon of AIOS infected blood with a needle. He called up his niggas. Dominique and Markel then were the only two people that got dirt on me. And I got dirt on them. It makes it that much better to do dirt with each other.

I called Markel, he picked up on the second ring. I told him the situation of how me, Lexus, and my son walked in the house, and the back door was halfway open. **"Damn home that fucked up." "Give me 20 minutes while I'm out running my sister to the doctor."** Once they hung up, Bohead called Dominique to let him know what went down to the being, a hothead like Bohead; it did take him 15 minutes to get to his partner. Bohead dropped Lexus and Lil Bohead at Lexus's momma's house while the three of them met at one of many spots they had around Nashville. The three of them got all the things they needed for the mission.

Bohead told them it might be a lot of people in the house, so grab some rope and duck tape. Markel got the gloves and the painting uniforms they were gonna wear. **"All yeah, I forgot to tell y'all, these obstacles gonna be real dragons on our end."** Markel and Dominique looked at each other in confusion. **"Why do you say that?"** They asked at the same time. **"Go look in the freezer. Get that blood and put it in some running hot water to melt it." "Where the fuck do you get a gallon of blood from?" "Nah, Markel, that's not the question. The question is what the fuck you got some blood for?"**

When Dominique got the blood out of the freezer, he didn't notice the tag hanging from the handle. Bohead walked to the sink and picked the jug up. He turned the tag around so the both of them could see. It read AIDS infected. They looked at Bohead with their mouth open. Not believing they just handled some AIDS-infected blood and knowing Bohead was crazy. See, murder was bred deep within Bohead. Dominique and Markel were committing the act of murder, but Bohead was a killer. He breathed murder.

It always went to a higher level with him. **"Bohead, you crazy man,"** Markel said, not being able to hold it any longer. Bohead burst into his signature laugh. **"Yeah, we will shoot the whole family up with AIDS." "Damn, Bohead, that's some cold-blooded shit, man." "Nigga I know you are not going soft on me nigga." "Nah, never that!" "Ok, let's roll out."** They pulled out in one of many vans that had different businesses painted on the side. This one said Will Paint in different colors, boldly printed.

When they pulled up at the house. The driveway was filled up. The yard even had cars parked in it. Bohead noticed it was a brand new hummer truck parked in front of the other cars. "Look." They couldn't wait to put down on something. The three of them looked around for any witnesses standing around. Then the three of them exited the van looking like three hard-working painters. Stains of all different colors were on their jeans and shirts. Markel had the daffy bag with the rope and duck tape etc… **"Nah, forget this; I got another plan."**

"Dominique, go secure the back door, and you, go make sure no one escape the side windows. This shouldn't take long." Bohead reached his pocket and pulled out four big 24oz cans, but there were super sleeping gas bombs. Bohead threw all four of them in the upstairs window. In just a few minutes, you could see the orange red smoke spread through the house.

You could hear the family members screaming. "Where the f**k is this smoke coming from? Then blum, blum, blum. They all feel some two at a time.

After waiting 10 minutes for the smoke to clear up, the three of them entered the house, with gloves on and all skin covered up. The gas only lasted an hour, so they had to get to work. Markel ran upstairs to find 3 people laid out. He grabbed two of them by their arms and dragged them downstairs while Bohead & Dominique had the rest of the family tied up to the chair. Markel ran back upstairs to get the last person. The other ones were on the crouch tied as if they were watching TV. The three of them grabbed a needle out of the daffy bag. Behead grabbed and opened up the gallon of blood. **"Here, dig in."** Dominique drew blood first, then Markel, and Bohead, last. **"Where should I start injecting the blood?"** Markel asks. **"Anywhere, fool." "Man, this shit feels weird."** "This shit here is not like pulling a trigger on a gun, fool."

"I got to give it to him, Bohead; this shit here got me sick to the stomach." "Ok, let's just hurry up and get it over with." Each of them went to different areas of the rooms.

They all picked the same spot to shoot the blood in, their neck to their surprise. It didn't take long to finish. One more thing Bohead did before walking out the door; with red sprayed paint, he sprayed a welcome to the AIDS Family on the wall with ha, ha, ha underneath. The three of them walked out optional life painters, not a trace of evidence left behind, after putting work on his family and money.

Now it was on; it didn't take him any time to get the streets back pumping. Bohead got down to the basis for real. The dope was so good. He notices how fast his crew is going through the bricks. Bohead wanted to see for himself. So, one day, he went to the store to buy some baking soda. He hasn't been in the kitchen in some years. He asks one of his homeboys where the hummer is at. Bohead put some old newspaper on the table and broke down a whole brick. He had a way of bagging the brick up, so if he decided to cook again, all he had to do was grab one of the packs without weighing it up again. Which was in different bags; each bag was 4inches a split, 4 and a half ounces. Bohead was putting Sosa to the test doing this.

Chapter Nine

He grabbed one of the 4in a split double bagged it. Sosa as he was about to smash the dope. Knock, knock, knock, **"Yo, get in the damn door before I put this shit on the stove." "Bohead, it's your cousin's Mike. Mike and Keke. "Ok, let them in."** Keke came in first, greeting Bohead. **"Mhen!!! That shit is potent."**

"I know this is that real fish scale. It has been moving so fast. I want to see how much it jumps without trying to get any extras." Fire **me up and get me a pot,"** Keke said. They looked at each other, already knowing what was on each other mind. It was a contest between the two of them. They always did that even though they were from different hoods. They had different plugs when one didn't have anything. They kept the money in the family. When the coke was real fish scale, Bohead would call him to let him know how the coke was, and clade wise. Both of them were cold in whipping coke. Whoever cracks came out the prettiest win. Mike walked into the kitchen with a penitentiary mug on his face. **"What's up cuz I haven't seen you in, what 11 or 12 years and you come in here like you want to rob the place."** Bohead teased. **"Nah, it ain't like that, Lil cuz." "You know I'm happy to be out." "I heard good things about you in the pen. That you were the man to see if you were a paper chaser." "Yeah, but for that reason, I keep my circle tight. Know what I mean. It's a bunch of snakes out here, Mike. Mike, you gonna have to keep your grass cut and your high beams on when you start getting money because you gonna get money if you stick with the fam." "That's real, Bohead; I'm gonna keep these words in mind." "Ok, that's enough talking. Let me whip this coke up." "How much is that, Lil cuz?" "A bird, I'm gonna let you have it.**

Welcome home, big cuz." Bohead grabbed the hammer again and got to something the dope down.

He then weighed up 2 ounces of baking soda and put it in the bag. He had the heat in between medium and high, so the water was already boiling. He put the dope in the Pyrex jar and placed it in the pot. Butterknife in one hand, spoon in the other. Bohead was a pro in cooking dope. He put a little water in the Pyrex, mixed it a little more, pulled it out, placed it in the microwave for 10 seconds, and then pulled it out. He mixed it with the butter knife again. He put it in for another 10 seconds and pulled it; he mixed it until it cooled off. **"It jumped cuz, look how thick it is? How much do you think it is?"**

"I'll give you 6 ounces." Bohead placed the jar in cold water for 3 min. He then tried to shake the dope loose, but it was too thick in the jar, so he had to cut it out with the butter knife. Bohead placed the dope on a dry tile, then placed it on the scale. **"Damn!"** Bohead said. **"How much do you get cos it is a quarter bird?" "This that dope!"** After seeing how good the dope really was, Bohead knew he could easily turn 300 birds to 600.

And that's exactly what he did. Chilling in their new downtown condo, watching TV.

Bohead couldn't believe what they did that morning made the world news. The whole family was in the coma crying. How could somebody do something so wicked? They showed the inside of the house. The wicked wall read, Welcome to the Aids Family. Red Cross was out there parked across the street.

The newsman appeared. **"Breaking news, it's been confirmed that somebody gassed their family and came in to shoot them up with AIDs. Whoever thought and did this must came from a horror movie. Because this is unbelievable, this kind of stuff only happens in movies."** Bohead grieved, turned off the TV and went on with his day's activity. The three of them were headed to Florida for business. The next morning, the three of them landed in Florida. Bohead knew he needed to take over a big piece of Florida drug trade. **"We need to hurry up and find a spot so Lexus can send our firepower; so that we can get a couple of suits. Yeah, let's do that."** That way, we won't have to wait on our guns. They drove around until they found a hotel all three of them liked.

The hotel was one that was overlooking the ocean. They got settled in three different rooms.

Even though they were down there for business purposes, Dominique and Markel were looking forward to other things taking place. They are always competing with each other. With the competition being that anyone who fucks the highest number of bitch wins. They would go through 3 or 4 bitches a night. It didn't matter how they got the pussy as long as they got it. **"What's up, Bohead, you in on this one? We up the price to 50,000. "Nah, I'm gonna chill out on this one. When we take a trip to Brazil, where the real bad bitches at, I'm gonna be in. Until then, y'all can have fun, fucking them ugly ass hoes y'all been picking."**

Bohead teased. **"When y'all get back, I want to talk to both of you about something important." "Tell me now, Bohead, if it's important, I want to know." "Listen, I know both of y'all have made a lot of money since we started the HGA cartel. We are brothers from another mother. If it wasn't for that, and knowing we might need each other** when it's all over." "When what's all over, Bohead?" Markel ask.

"Selling dope nigga! Out here putting our lives on the line for these millions, soon to be billions." "Where are you driving at, homie?" "The getting is good right now, but it probably won't be for long. So put some of the money in some legal shit. Y'all feel me?" "Yeah, we feel you, homie, always keeping the team on point," Dominique said, speaking up for both of them.

"Come on, let's roll," Bohead said, ready to club. The three of them hit the scene hard. The girls were all on them, looking, pointing, and smiling. The three of them smelled like money. They looked at each other, knowing the chase wasn't gonna be hard. "So what's up, let's get one of them booth over there. Get a few bottles of rose and let the game begins."

Markel and Dominique went their separate ways while Bohead sat in the booth, scanning his surroundings. He noticed a few niggas carrying themselves like money. He knew it wasn't all fun and games. You had to do your homework to last in this game of chess. Bohead knew other niggas are playing checkers, and it won't be hard to checkmate their ass.

It didn't take Dominique long to snag him a thick dark skin chick. Markel saw what he always had across the room. He yelled out his name. **"Dominique! Dominique!"** Dominique turned around and spotted Markel standing at the bar with a tall amazon light skin chick.

Markel put his bottle down on the bar and threw up, letting him know he was a point short from a dime piece. Dominique shook him off. He decided to go and lay it down for the night. An hour later, Markel and his amazon were on their way back to the hotel. Bohead stayed a little longer waiting on one of his victims to leave.

"Damn," he said, noticing two bad Latinos walking his way. **"Hey, papi, you look boring seating over here all by yourself. Can my sister and I sit down and drink with you?" Yeah, but you two better not be on some shiest shit. I'm shell shock, get shot, or slow your roll. No, papi, we are just looking to have a good time. What kind of time?"**

"A good time." Bohead laughed, knowing exactly what he wanted to do with the both of them. **"Ok, we gonna do it like this; give me a number to call."** They wrote down a number and handed it to him. I'm waiting on somebody. You two grab a bottle each and go party. They did what they were told.

Bohead watched as they walked off to see if any nigga was trying to scope him out. Bohead disappeared into the crowd and out the door. He entered the hotel lobby and called the two girls. In a few seconds, he watched the two walk toward the hotel. The two of them were bad. I mean with a hair damn bad.

They entered the hotel, still drinking on the Rose. The three of them headed to the room, knowing it was about to go down like downtown on the fourth of July. Soon as they entered the room, they got to take off their clothes, kissing and grabbing each other only where a man was supposed to. Damn was the only thing that came out of Bohead's mouth when he saw one lay down on her back while the other one stood over her in a sitting position fingering herself.

"Come for me mami. "Ooh, I'm gonna come for you."

"Lick this pussy." She sucked and licked on that pussy like a pro. "Mami, this pussy tastes like banana pudding." "It's good, ain't it?" She was nodding her face like she was on top of a dick. "Ooh, mami, I'm about to cum. Ooh, here I cum." The both of them were moaning. The one lying down shook a finger in her pussy; when she pulled out, a big splash came running out her pussy. "Ooh, mami, that pussy came hard."

Bohead said with his dick in his hand. He walked over to the bed and stuck his dick in both of their mouths. He pulled out of one and stuck it in the other one. "Damn, y'all Latinos freaky. "Ym, hm, we are. We like turning out fine niggas like you." "That's enough talking; get back to sucking on this hard dick." Papi, I want to fuck it?" "Come on, bend over then." He stuck his dick in the one that was sucking on the other bitch's pussy. It got so wet, so fast that it was splashing out juice. "Come on, papi, hit this pussy." Bohead got to hitting it rough and fast. "Ooh, papi, just like that, I'm cuming, daddy." She came all over his dick. When

Bohead pulled out, his dick was fucking wet. **"Come on, papi, I want some of that dick too."** Bohead laid on his back because he was out of breath a little. She got on top of him and slid down slow so he could feel every muscle inside of her. He couldn't help it. Bohead had to say it again. **"Damn, you Latinos got some fine pussy." "You like it, papi? It can be all of yours if you want it."** Bohead didn't say anything. He just kept on fucking her fine ass.

"Watch out, mami, I'm about to cum. You gonna swallow it?" "Yeah," she said. **"I want to taste it,"** the other said. Bohead pushed her off him to stand up. He squirted in both of their mouths. After all that hardcore fucking, they were tired, so the three of them went to sleep. Bohead woke up from a few knocks on the door. **"Who is it?" "Nigga it's Dominique and Markel." Hold on, let me put some clothes on. Yo, you two, wake up; my homies are about to come in. Go in there to freshen up."** Bohead wanted to show them off to his homies. He opened the door to see four people standing in front of him.

The two of them still had three girls they had just met last night. It was a surprise to Bohead because usually, his niggas would've already sent them by the way. **"What's up, homies?" "We had to come check on you. I told Dominique it was a lot of noise from this side of the hallway last night. She'd, I would've already been pronounced dead."**

"I see now that my life ain't worth more than a piece of good pussy to y'all." Bohead said, teasing his homies. **"Nah, homie, you know it ain't nowhere near like that with us,"** Dominique said, speaking up for the both of them. **"So, what's up with the four of you this morning?" These 2 bitches right here, you know we got 50,000 on which one is the baddest. We need you on this one. Just keep it real."** Now, which one would you want to fuck first? Just as Bohead was about to choose one, both of the Latinos came walking from the back. **"Damn, Bohead, I see you came up last night. Y'all niggas are something else these days. You got a bitch standing right here next to you that you happen to fuck last night, and you right here giving the next two bitches props on how good they look?"**

That turned Dominique on. Knowing she was a standup type of girl. **"My fault; I didn't know you were gonna take it so personal with my niggas going soft on a female." "Damn, what is the world coming to?"** Markel said, teasing his homies. **"Well, it looks to me like you won the 50,000 out of his pocket." "Nah, y'all keep the money. I got enough of that. Put it on my tab. I might need y'all in the near future. That's called collator. Anyway, I saw a few niggas in the club last night. That could be moving a lil something, something down here. We gonna have to find them and have a talk with them about our HGA movement." "How are you planning on getting in touch with any hustlers down here in Florida?"** One of the Latinos asked as she overheard Bohead's conversation. **"What is your name anyway?" "My name is Christina and hers, Mania." "Damn, Bohead, you got these two females in the room, and you just findings out their names now."**

"We weren't about all that last night. They wanted to have a good time. So that's exactly what I gave them." "When should the package be here?" "Any time today. I

guess after all the wild talking last night, you ready to get down to business?"** Bohead ask. **"And you know it. That's when I go the hardest. And it seems like the niggas get down faster."** Dominique responded. **"Hey, papi, whatever you do, my sister and I want to be down."** The older one asks. **"We could be a lot of help for the HGA movement. "Why do you think you would be of any use for our movement?" "Don't let the pretty nice body fool y'all." "Well, I can see we did that already." "My big sister and I hit a woman. A lot of guys down here in Florida pay us to kill people." "Stop lying!"** Markel said, not believing what he had just heard. **"There ain't no way that two fine ass Latinos could have such an ugly way of living."**

"Well, it's true." The younger sister said with much, much sadness in her voice. **"So y'all sure you both want to be in this HGA movement?" "Yes." "Come on, let's go talk this shit over some grubs."** Dominique and Markel got a contact number from their duties and dismissed them like they were teachers in a 12th-grade class.

The two girls were pissed because they couldn't come along for breakfast. Dominique and Markel didn't give a fuck. It was BOB with them. Business over Bitches, but it wouldn't be right if they didn't hand over a few notes. So they gave them 500 pieces after waiting on his homie's confirmation with the females. The five of them headed to their destination, which was a downstairs restaurant. The five of them found a table in the corner of the dinner so other customers couldn't hear the conversation they were about to have. Bohead called a waitress over so they could order.

"Give me the supreme omelet with a large orange juice." "Give us the same thing he got." The bigger sister spoke up. **"What y'all two niggas want?"** They were busy staring at the Latinos. Markel ordered first. **"Give me 3 pancakes with eggs on the side with a large orange juice." "And give me the same thing with sausages on the side."** Bohead got right to it. He spoke firmly, **"Listen, girls, this is a great opportunity for the both of you. If y'all are down to work hard and go hard. We'll make sure y'all are rich in a couple of years. I might decide to recruit**

yall. The three of us gonna have to be ready. We gonna give y'all half the money upfront and the other half when we know the job was done. But first, y'all gonna have to show us how you two get down." "So, what are you asking for?" Show me how violent two beautiful Latinos can get." Ok, you want us to get down with that?" The younger sister pulled out a pen and pad and wrote something down. She folded the note and handed it to Bohead. All talking ceased when the waitress was seen walking toward the table with the food.

After eating, the two Latinos said goodbye to go get on their mission. Bohead didn't know that he had found two loyal Lations that only wanted to be part of something in their lifetime. They were down to do whatever their bloodline went to way back in the day. Their father branded them to be what they are, but they were only supposed to kill if a boyfriend or a husband got out of line. As they got older, the youngest one came up with a meaningful plan. And that was to make money from killing. The only people they wouldn't kill were women or kids. Christina was so evil she would give her nieces and nephews serial killer tips.

And Maria she had no conscience; she was a psychopath. And she thought that was so cute about what her nieces and nephews were learning. Christina and Maria were going out to find a 35-year-old drug dealer. They were gonna cut off patches of his flesh and leave him naked, propped up by a dumpster with a bullet in his head.

Chapter Ten

Bohead, Dominique and Markel were on their way back to their room. Until they saw Fed-ex pull up to the hotel door. The driver got out the truck with a large box and put it on some type of stretcher, but before he made it to the door, the three of them were already on his tail. **"Yo Fed-ex man?"** The guy looked around to see where the voice came from. Bohead was already up on him, about to tap on the guy shoulder, but the guy turned around and jumped!"

"Damn man, you scared the shit out of me, man!" Bohead could tell the nigga was hood because he had a mouth full of gilds. **"What**

are you scared of? Ain't nothing gonna happen to you in front of all these people." "You should never know these days. I have only been working for about a year and a half, and I can tell you in the same place I was in. So I know you know how it feels when you have done something to a lot of people." "Yeah, that shit hunts you for the rest of your life." "Well, I came over here to see what that package has for me." "The name on the package says Julius." "That's me." That's cool; if you weren't staying in this building, I could give it to you. If I give this package to you and you have a room here, you won't be able to take it up if the front lieutenant hasn't checked it in."

"Don't worry about that; it's mine, so it's going to the room with me regardless." He gave the package to Bohead without any other problems. He didn't even have to sign any papers. Even if he did, Bohead wasn't putting his name on anything. Not until everything he was into was legit. He gave the front lieutenant 500 dollars for a clear path to his room with his packages. The three of them went to Bohead's room. Lexus said she had got some new firepower from Gun city, and the three of them wanted to know what they were packing.

Bohead opened the box. It was filled with boxes of bullets, guns, and three bulletproof vests. Bohead laid everything on the bed. **"What y'all think about these?" "What have we got here?" "We've got 3 street sweeper shotguns and 3 baby FN 502 plus 3 ankle holsters." "With all this, I'm ready to put in some work!"** Markel said with the calico in his hands. They all got to suit it and boot it. Bohead called Lexus to let her know that he just got the package, and they were on their way out to take what's the HGA cartel.

They told each other that they loved one another, and the call ended. The three of them got in the car. Dominique brought his very own navigation system so it won't be hard getting from destination and other locations around Florida. **"Listen, Dominique, you know how we do things,** Bohead said, **but we gonna do it different on this round. Y'all know, at first, we always pick the lil young niggas on the blocks starveling and give them the work on consignment. But we got too much coke to be doing it like that right now. We are going after the big drug dealers**

by moving 50 kilos or more. The same rule applies; you gonna get down, or you gonna lay down and if you lay down, you staying down." "So, Bohead, how do you plan on seeing these types of guys?" It's all types of ways, one, we gonna roll up on a few dope streets. Give the lil niggas or whoever is out there serving out numbers. And tell them we need a call from their supplier in 24 hours."

"If that doesn't work, we gonna ride up on some niggas riding real nice. On some 3os or some type of family car. Niggas down here like to show off. They did just that. Rode around Florida, letting niggas know it was three new niggas in town with the coke." Bohead noticed on some of the dude's faces that it wouldn't gonna be that easy taking over a block that they have been on all their life. But they had another thing coming.

HGA cartel was coming full speed ahead with no brakes. They are either gonna ride or get rode over and put in a buddy bag. They were back at the hotel around 6.00 that morning. The three of them were tired than a mother fucker. All they wanted was some rest after all the driving around in the car that was rented. But it wasn't even half the work they were gonna have to put in.

The location they were in was Palm Beach; tomorrow was gonna be the city of Miami. When they finally went to their rooms, almost immediately getting in their room, all three of them went to sleep.

"Yo homie, what the fuck are you sitting on my car for?" "Then I still, you are about sitting on my car like 3 days ago." Bohead got up from watching to see what was all the commotion outside, getting closer to the two niggas arguing. One of them was Bohead's cousin, Keke. **"Keke, what's going on? Why are you out here snapping? I then told this nigga to stop sitting on my ride; he's been hard heading. He's gonna make me do something to him." "Yo buddy, I don't take threats lightly, so you really need to watch your mouth when you talk to me."**

By then, two of his homies were walking up on the commotion, and from the look of it, they had guns on them and wasn't looking for any peace treatment. Bohead, on seeing what was about to go down, pulled out his blue steel 45 ammunition and tried to fire off a few shots. **"Damn, my gun then jammed on me, cuz**." Keke pulled out his extra gun and threw it to Bohead, but before he could get the gun in position to shoot. He was hit two times in the chest and twice in the stomach. Bohead was so hell shocked from getting shot; the only thing that came to mind was to run, and that's exactly what he did. The shooting finally came to an end, and the street was clear as Windex cleared mirror.

Bohead was coming face to face with life itself. Everything that he ever did was flashing in his face. People that he loved and cared for was looking and crying over him. **"What's going on? Momma, why are you crying?"** Bohead looked around and noticed that nobody could hear what he was saying. Then everything Bohead had and brought was flashing in his face. He noticed he was walking around in a beautiful house. It was a huge mansion, but something was up with that. I never bought a mansion. Then all of a sudden, a familiar face came to view. He said, if you believe in me, let go. I didn't say anything. I let go. I was gonna fall into something, and it was a very, very long way down. I looked back at the familiar face, then I came to my decision, and I grabbed one of these chains. And that's what Bohead did. I wanted to know where and what I was falling into, but that's only lasted for a second. Then I let go again. It was over. "I'm gonna see y'all later," was the last word I spoke to my loved ones.

Bohead couldn't believe what was happening to him. He woke up, heart racing and face sweating. **"Damn, only a dream. My mind must be playing tricks on me again."** Bohead said, thinking out loud to himself. But one thing was worrying Bohead. Tricks are for kids, and I was far from a kid. Bohead thought hard about the dream. Knowing that it was part of his life was gonna have to come to an end.

"But for right now, I'm gonna stay on my paper chase. I got plans for my crew." Bohead knew his homies weren't up yet. He walked down to the restaurant for a private breakfast. That dream had him worried. It wasn't the first time he had had a dream that he had been shot. Was it a sign telling him to slow his roll. One thing Bohead always did was take signs seriously. It could cost him his life.

Thinking about his life, Bohead decided to call Christina and Maria. He wanted to know if they were capable of working their way into his life. If the mission wasn't completed today, Bohead plans on cutting them loose. The dream really got him paranoid. They could be out to kill him. **"Listen, which one of you am I talking to?" "This is Christina, papi." "What's the business on y'all end? Have the two of you take care of that yet?" "No, not yet." She said in her Spanish voice. "Well, if it's not taken care of today, I won't be needing y'all on this journey of mine." Bohead was serious. "Papi, later on, tonight, look at the news; we want to be down. Have you read the paper I gave you at breakfast?" "Not at all, not yet." Well, when the news comes on, read it. And you will know the mission is complete."** Bohead could really tell the two girls wanted to be down. She was really wining on the phone. Usually, Latinos came on starring.

Bohead went back up to Dominique's and Markel's room to get the both of them up. They have been sleeping long enough. **"Knock,**

knock, knock." "Who is it? I didn't order any room service. Who could be knocking on my door this early? "Nigga, this Bohead. Open the door." Hold on for a second, let me put my gun down." Dominique put his gun down back under his pillow and opened the door for Bohead. **"What's up nigga? You still in here sleeping?"**

"Yeah, nigga, we clocked in major hours yesterday. It's too damn early to be up." "It's never too early for me." "My motto is the early bird catch the worm. I didn't come this far for nothing." Yeah, to nigga getting lazy. "Have you heard anything from the two Latinos?" Yeah I talked to them a few minutes ago." "You know I had to put some --- on them." "What do you mean by that?" I told them if the job wasn't done today, we don't need them." "Come on, put some clothes on so we can go wake Markel up." It didn't take Dominique any time to get dressed. In just a few seconds, they were walking out the door. **"Markel had to be sky high from last night. He knew we had some business to handle."**

"We would hear it from the hallway." "Knock, knock." **"Who is it?** Dominique and Bohead walks to the door to see who it was together. Bohead opens the door for his homies." **Damn nigga why you got the TV so loud?"** We could hear that motherfucker in the hallway. Dominique told him." Even though we love each other, it was always something to fight about." **Man fucks how loud the TV is" "Let's go out to lay some nigga out." My phone hasn't ringed yet. "Them niggas didn't take us seriously. "Come on, let's go,"** Bohead said.

The 3 of them got in the B.D.M an all-black work van with different magnets stating the business carpet cleaning, pressure washing, lawn care, car detail and house repair. But that was far from what the van was used for. Bohead was creative when it was time to put in some work.

The element of surprise on each victim that fell for the fake carpet cleaning business. Every new mission is always a different job. We even get the van wrapped in different colors.

We had to go hunt the drug dealers down about our paper. Every crew in the city had to give us a piece of every sale, the deal they did, or it won't be any peace.

This last crew was giving us a hard time about their money. It was nothing Bohead could not handle. He had it all figured out.

He found out where the headman of the crew lives at. The mission was gonna play out like this. Bohead, Markel and Dominique were going back on the door to see if he would like their service. Once someone answers the door, it will be all game from there.

The neighborhood Max Jacob lived in was beautiful. All the estates had 5 acres or more land. Every lawn was at their best.

Because of the long ride thing in Jacob's neighborhood, we were able to witness the heaven of a place. This neighborhood was heaven on Earth.

As the trace at us approached Jacob's estate, Dominique noticed it was common all around the estate. **"No problem,"** Bohead said. Bohead reached in a duffle bag he had with him. He pulled out 3 white man masks he had made. He did give them to his partners. **"Here, put this on."**

Bohead, Dominique, and Markel were now ready to knock on Jacob's door. Once the mission is completed, and the police check the camera system. A warrant for 3 white young men will be issued. It will be all over the news. Those 3 white young men did a home invasion which left a whole family murdered.

Even though Dominique was a gangster, he had faith in God. So Dominique stated that we should pray before knocking on the door. **"Pray!"** Bohead said. **"Pray!"** Markel said, too. "Yeah, I just do not feel right with this mission."

Having been friends as long as they have, they all put their heads down and said a prayer.

It was now time. The doorbell had been ringed; a beautiful maid could be seen walking toward the door. **"May I help you?"** She said with the door halfway opened. **"Yes, you can, beautiful—we are a new company out looking for business. B.D.M offer great service. Carpet cleaning, pressure washing, lawn care, and more."**

Before the maid could say not B any of our services. Bohead was upping his pistol pushing through the door. What Bohead didn't notice was the maid was reaching for her pistol. Markel gave her a headshot. "**One down; how many left to go,**" Dominique said.

"**Whatever it may take to get to the money,**" Markel said back.

Jacob heard all the commotion from the upper room. He had been training his family for home invasion situations for years. It was go time for them too. He had an escape route at the second level of his estate. The only problem he had was that his kids were downstairs in their rooms.

All of them were in their room playing on the internet. That Tic-Tok, Instagram, and Facebook got our kids grouping off artificial intelligence.

But not mine; all my kids had been trained Military style from a real Navy Seal. All the rooms downstairs had semi-automatics in them.

Once Bohead, Markel, and Dominique entered one of the kids' rooms, the child just looked at them and kept playing. Bohead walked to the child to tie her up, but it went down from there. Once Bohead reached for her, she pulled out a baby glock. POW, POW, POW, Bohead was shot all 3 times, one time in the neck and twice in the head. Bohead Paid for His Own Funeral will be continued.

UNITED STATES
OF AMERICA
MK 305753

www.ingramcontent.com/pod-product-compliance
Lightning Source LLC
Chambersburg PA
CBHW071433300726

48976CB00004B/1316